KU-511-228

UNION
OF ANGOLA
VETERANS

Russian Veterans of Angola:
from the Past to Nowadays

PHOTO ALBUM

2020

Kolomnin S., Balakleyev S.
Russian Veterans of Angola: from the Past to Nowadays.
Photo album / Compiled by Sergei Kolomnin, Sergei Balakleyev.
Moscow, Ethnica Studio Publishers (Troshkov A. V. individual enterprise), 2020

ISBN 978-5-6045476-1-8

Did we really need everything what Soviet military and civil specialists were doing in Angola in 1970–90ies? The Russian Union of Angola Veterans believes that it was imperative, that our efforts were not futile. Due to Soviet and Cuban assistance in 1970–90ies Angola secured its sovereignty, independence and territorial integrity, and today it is a friendly African country both to Russia and Cuba. In Angola every one in his own capacity – a serviceman, diplomat, doctor, builder, geologist and fisherman – they were all doing one and the same great and important job: they assisted the people of the country to build a new state. The Russian Union of Angola Veterans carefully cherishes the memory of those events.

You are holding a publication with a collection of unique historic photographs illustrating the work of our specialists in Angola in 1970–90ies as well as images displaying today's activities of the Union in Russia and abroad.

ISBN 978-5-6045476-1-8

© Kolomnin Sergei Anatolyevich, 2020
© Balakleyev Sergei Aleksandrovich, 2020
© Design: Ethnica studio, 2020

Central monument of the memorial
"To Cuito Cuanavale Defenders"[1],
Angola, Cuando Cubango Province.
Photo: A. Stvolin

This is the photo album published by the Union of Angola Veterans *From the Past to Nowadays*. It is composed of two parts: one is devoted to the history and events in Angola in 1970–90ies which our countrymen were part of, the second speaks of the present.

More than forty years have passed since many of the presented retro photographs had been first published. Those are not just images from the previous century, those are pictures of a different epoch. At that time many Soviet citizens wherever they may be living – European part of Russia, Ukraine, Siberia or Far East – were the children of their times and country, and nearly all were internationally-minded people. That was the way we were brought up... We strongly believed in the ideals of justice, equality and fraternity, and many of us were ready, if called upon by the national leaders, to rush to the world's end to protect or help anyone in need to restore justice usurped by the enemy.

This is what happened in Angola. No sooner the country had been born and declared its independence Angola became a victim of an armed aggression by the Republic of Zaire and South Africa which illegally occupied neighboring Namibia. At the request of the MPLA party which came to power in Angola the Soviet Union and Cuba sent its citizens to the country to help Angolans in repelling the armed aggression and building up of a new army, in restoring national economy devastated by the war. Our specialists detailed to Angola also rendered assistance to SWAPO fighters from Namibia and activists of the African National Congress from South Africa who found refuge in Angola – subject to SA harassment and oppression because of their struggle against apartheid, for freedom and independence of their countries.

Angolan Mi-24 helicopters of Soviet production over
Serra da Leba pass, Lubango-Namibe road.
A winding highway going downhill from the Serra da Leba
mountain is one of Angola's national symbols

Carrying out their service and internationalist duty, our military advisers, specialists and interpreters were part of combat units of the Angolan army and SWAPO armed units. They both trained soldiers and often directly participated in combat operations fighting shoulder-to-shoulder with Angolan, Cuban and Namibian combatants. Together with the Angolans our civil specialists were building power stations, houses, bridges, roads, giving medical assistance to people, participating in restoration of the fishing fleet, mastering the fundamentals of government administration.

Over the years of cooperation between the USSR/Russia and Angola (1975–1992) about 100 thousand Soviet and Russian citizens came to work in Angola. They accomplished their service and internationalist duty with flying colors. Many of them sincerely gave their hearts to this country and its people and continue to maintain close ties with Angola till now.

A public organization of the participants of international assistance to the Republic of Angola – the Union of Angola Veterans – was established in Russia in 2004. It was founded by activists who never sought any personal benefits. Those were the people who considered their work in Angola to be a personal human mission. Till nowadays this understanding allows to actively employ the potential of Union members in performing one of the key provisions of the Union's Statute: to contribute to the development of public, cultural and economic relations with the Republic of Angola. The second part of the album is devoted to those efforts.

The Union of Angola Veterans is based on the membership of all categories of specialists engaged in international assistance, participants of combat operations in that number. It incorporates retired servicemen – military advisers and interpreters – and civilians – diplomats of all ranks, bridge builders, medical doctors, pilots, fishermen, agriculturists, civil engineers, geologists and representatives of other professions.

The Angolans very well remember those who helped the young republic to survive and win under pressure of systematic aggressions of South Africa where the white authorities pursued the inhuman policy of apartheid. When meeting a delegation of the Russian Union of Angola Veterans in November 2015 future President of the Republic of Angola, at that time Minister of Defense, João Lourenço explicitly described the importance of Angolan-Soviet relations to Angola and the role of Soviet and Russian military and civil specialists.

"Today we welcome Russian war veterans. I want to emphasize strongly that they are not veterans of their own war but specifically our war, the war for national liberation and sovereignty of Angola, and we are sincerely grateful for that. Today Angola attaches special importance to its relations with Russia, the successor of the USSR, with the country which offered invaluable support in winning our independence in November 1975 and then rendered vast assistance in our struggle against Zairean invaders and aggressors of South African apartheid. Eventually, with this assistance we managed to defeat the SA Army though at that time it was pronounced "the invincible". I can't find words to express my gratitude. Due to the assistance of the Soviet Union and Russia Angola managed to overcome the subsequent internal military conflict. Today we firmly stand on our both feet, not in the least due to your assistance both in the past and at present".

The photo album of the Russian Union of Angola Veterans *From the Past to Nowadays* contains more than two hundred fifty unique photographs illustrating both the efforts of Soviet and Russian specialists in Angola in 1970–90ies and images showing current activities of the Union.

Angolan and Soviet officers carry out reconnaissance before an operation against UNITA[2] under the code name "Zebra" in the area of the command post of the 59th FAPLA[3] Mechanized Infantry Brigade, Cuando Cubango Province. In the center: Head of the Operations Department of FAPLA General Staff Gen Roberto Monteiro "Ngongo" and acting Chief Military Adviser (CMA)[4] Lt Gen Valery Belyaev with military interpreter Maj Sergei Antonov. 1989. Photo: S. Antonov

Angola Is Part of Our Memory and Our History

★1

★2

★3

★1. Angola is the place where we do our military service.
Operations officer-on-duty in the Russian military mission
at the headquarters of the Southern Front Lt Col Vadim Sagachko
at the map of Angola. 1990. Lubango. Photo: V. Sagachko

★2. President of Angola Agostinho Neto on board the large
landing ship[5] *Krasnaya Presnya* visiting Luanda seaport.
On the left is the Chief Military Adviser in Angola Gen Major
Ilya Ponomarenko, to the right – Commander of the ship's
landing crew Major Sergei Remizov. 1977. Photo: S. Remizov

★3. Political briefing under field conditions. The duties of our military
advisers in Angola were not limited to combat training but also
included daily briefing about events in the country and abroad.
Maj Vladimir Soldatchenko addresses the Angolans, to the right –
military interpreter. 1984. Mulongo. Photo: V. Soldatchenko

Defending their Motherland "in the far reaches", in 1975–1992 on the invitation of the sovereign government several dozens thousand military advisers, specialists and interpreters, naval mariners and military pilots were stationed in Angola. Thousands of civil specialists – medical doctors, civil engineers, surveyors, teachers, fishermen, agriculturists, bridge-builders and representatives of other professions helped to restore civil infrastructure and build new industrial enterprises.

In 1975–1991 the 10th Chief Department of the General Staff alone sent about 12 thousand Soviet servicemen (among them 107 generals and admirals, 7 211 officers, more than 3.5 thousand WOs, privates and civilian employees of the Soviet Army and Navy) to help Angola in building up its national army and repelling outside aggression. All in all about 40 thousand servicemen were sent on a mission to Angola during the aforementioned period who helped in shaping the national army of Angola and armed forces of SWAPO (PLAN) and military wing of the ANC. Among them 834 servicemen were decorated with the state awards of the USSR for their military service in Angola, including those decorated with state orders – 580 servicemen, 274 were decorated with state medals.

The scale of presence of civil specialists in Angola is also impressive: in the mid-80ies the Trade Representative of the USSR in Angola instantaneously employed about three thousand experts. The spectrum of the duties of specialists dispatched to Angola was really vast. They assisted in creating a national system of health care and education, transportation and housing infrastructure, together with the Angolans restored merchant navy and fishing fleet, worked as rank-and-file doctors in hospitals and clinics, repaired Soviet aircraft and motor vehicles, restored bridges destroyed by South African troops.

A special mission was assigned to the Navy mariners. The ships of the Soviet Navy stationed at the shores of Angola carried out both their duty of military service in the interests of the country and protected our merchant fleet, escorted heavy-lift cargo ships with important goods and war materials forwarded from the Soviet Union and Cuba to Angola and other countries. Besides, those combat ships were commissioned to support the MPLA government in case of a crisis and evacuation of Soviet citizens or a threat to the lives of our compatriots. In 1975–76 ships of the Soviet Navy escorted and protected Soviet and Cuban vessels carrying troops and war equipment from Cuba to assist the MPLA movement and Angolan government in repelling the Zairean and SA aggression (Cuban operation "Carlota"). All Soviet combat ship commanders were assigned a mission of counter sabotage, protection and defense of Soviet fishing vessels both at sea and during high sea fishing, as well as moorage in Angolan seaports.

Pilots of the Air Force were also of great help. Between 1976–1990 Soviet An-12 and Il-76 military cargo aircraft organic to the CMA's air wing were the tip of the military spear of Angolan AF transport aviation. They ensured both transportation of Soviet military personnel and carried out a considerable part of cargo delivery to the Angolan government forces (FAPLA) and Cuban troops.

Soviet military advisers and specialists taught Angolan commanders to plan and conduct the battle both in the offensive and defense, proper escort of cargo convoys, minefield laying and demining, conduct of reconnaissance, adequate maintenance of combat equipment. They taught their craft to pilots, tank-men and naval mariners. Our specialists rendered invaluable assistance in repair and maintenance of Soviet war equipment. Many advisers often became number-two (assistant) members of the crew of Angolan commanders, their "shadow" of sorts. At the time of joint combat operations they had to take assault rifles and machine guns in their hands, drive APCs and handle control levers of tanks, operate fire control consoles of missile and AA means.

Those were true military professionals who contributed much to the construction of Angolan Armed Forces. The fact that since mid-80ies the Angolan Army has begun "to cope" with the most combat-effective army in Africa, South African Defence Force, practically on an equal footing was an outstanding achievement of thousands of Soviet officers and generals who worked in Angola.

Photographs presented in the first part of the photo album show the efforts of our compatriots assigned to Angola in 1975–1992 to assist the nation.

★4

★6

★5

★4. A group of Soviet civil surveyors and geodesists with the Institute for Geodesy and Cartography of Angola take a picture at a bridge across the Cuanza River together with Angolan guards. 1980. Photo: N. Simakov (standing third from the right)

★5. A group of Soviet civil bridge-building specialists with the National bridge construction enterprise of Angola (ENP) together with SWAPO fighters[6] safeguarding the Lubango-Moçâmedes road (Serra da Leba pass). When travelling to dangerous areas civil specialists were obliged to carry small arms. 1984. Photo: S. Kononov (sitting second from the right)

★6. A group of military advisers awaiting embarkation on An-12 aircraft (Chief Military Adviser's air wing[7]) due to Luanda. 1984. Lubango. Photo: V. Soldatenko (extreme right)

★7. President José Eduardo dos Santos on a visit to *Tallin*, a Soviet large anti-submarine ship[8], in the seaport of Luanda. Center (from left to right): commanding officer Capt 2nd rank Yu. Ustimenko, President of Angola, USSR Ambassador in Luanda V. Loginov, MPLA Politbureau Member L. Lara, Angola Minister of Defense P. Pedalé, Chief Military Adviser in Angola Lt Gen G. Petrovsky. 1981. Photo: Union of Angola Veterans archives

★8. Underwater counter sabotage. Landing force commander (*Krasnaya Presnya* large landing ship) Major Sergei Remizov in preparation to diving and inspection of the vessel's bottom. 1977. Luanda. Photo: S. Remizov

★9. Chief Military Adviser in Angola (1977–1980) Lt Gen V. Shakhnovich (third from the left) speaking with an Angolan commander (interpreter in the center). 1978. Photo: V. Shakhnovich

★10. Military training center at Menongue. Military interpreter Capt Pavel Akimov (second from the right) with FAPLA fighters at special armored fighting vehicles. 1990. Photo: V. Sagachko

★10

★**11.** USSR Ambassador in Angola Vladimir Kazimirov welcomes naval personnel of *Smyshlenyi* large anti-submarine ship performing alert patrol in the Atlantic Ocean within the 30th Operations Brigade[9] of the USSR Navy and visiting Luanda to replenish material supplies. 1987. Angola naval base. Photo: L. Sukhanov

★**12.** Repairs on our own. A Soviet officer with the Angolan Navy repairs a bus used by our advisors to move across Luanda. The majority of drivers of such vehicles were chosen from the ranks of Soviet military advisers[10], which became an additional unpaid job. 1987. Angola naval base. Photo: A. Korotkov

★**13.** The crew disembarking from the Tu-95RTs[11] reconnaissance plane (USSR Navy AF) after landing at Luanda airfield. Early 80ies. Photo: Ye. Kalinin

★14

★16

★15

★17

★18

★19

★14. Military interpreter Sen Lt Igor Sechin with an airfield guard at Namibe. In the background: Soviet An-12 cargo aircraft (CMA's air wing) refueling at Sonangol national oil company station. 1985. Photo: I. Sechin

★15. A Soviet military adviser gives instructions to the reconnaissance company of the 19th FAPLA Infantry Brigade before going on a mission. 1984. Mulondo. Photo: V. Soldatenko

★16. Meeting a group of Soviet KGB officers at the airport of Lubango who arrived to render assistance to their Angolan colleagues from the Ministry of State Security. 1989. Photo: S. Shuvanov (extreme right)

★17. At the Humpata training center firing range. Armor specialist Maj Orest Korgut at the T-55 tank upon a month-long training of Angolan tankmen (2nd FAPLA Infantry Brigade). 1982. Photo: O. Korgut

★18. Visiting the operational site. A working group of the Soviet GHQ officers headed by Army Gen V. Varennikov (second from the left, next to Col Gen K. Kurochkin) which arrived to assist the FAPLA command in repulsing the on-coming invasion of South African troops. 1986. Southern Angola. Photo: Union of Angola Veterans archives

★19. "Sovhispan"[12] has come! Soviet military specialists organic to the FAPLA tactical field group advancing on Mavinga receiving foodstuffs delivered by the Sovhispan company. Among Soviet officers – Sergei Mishchenko and Yury Lokotkov. Photo: S. Mishchenko

★**20.** Adviser of the Angolan MiG-21 air squadron commander Lt Col Vyacheslav Samoilov (center) after a training sortie with an Angolan pilot on MiG-21bis plane. 1985. Namibe airfield. Photo: V. Samoilov

★**21.** In a tour across the country a group of Angolan students of Soviet military academies[13] visited Leningrad (now – St. Petersburg). In the center – a student of the Moscow Military and Political Academy named after V. I. Lenin, now President of the Republic of Angola João Manuel Gonçalves Lourenço. 1981. Photo: I. Korolev (left from Lourenço)

★**22.** The first President of independent Angola Agostinho Neto views the Yak-38 VTOL fighter on board of *Minsk*, Soviet heavy aircraft-carrying cruiser visiting Luanda. April 2, 1977. Photo: Union of Angola Veterans archives

★21

★20

18

★24

★25

★23. Senior interpreter-desk officer of the CMA's Office in Angola Lt Col Viktor Belyukin demonstrates a French APILAS rocket anti-tank launcher captured in combat with UNITA troops. 1987. Photo: Union of Angola Veterans archives

★24. Warrant officer Nikolai Pestretsov[14], a specialist in motor vehicle repair of the 11th FAPLA Infantry Brigade (left), on his way to the frontline together with Angolan fighters. 1981. Onjiva. Photo: Union of Angola Veterans archives

★25. The Battle for Cuito Cuanavale. Soviet military specialists: A. Moskvin (interpreter), S. Chernenkiy, M. Gribkov, V. Mozolev, V. Ilyin, V. Bitaev on board a BTR-60PB APC. May 1, 1987. Photo: V. Bitaev

★26. Back home! A Soviet military adviser collecting his sparse belongings before returning back home upon accomplishing his internationalist mission in the Angolan trenches. 1987. Cuito Cuanavale. Photo: S. Mishchenko

★26

★27

★28

★29

★**27.** Namibian SWAPO (PLAN) fighters[15] stationed in Angola perform live firing from Grad-P rocket launcher. 1985. Namib Desert. Photo: V. Stryukov

★**28.** Soviet military advisers with the Angolan AA Brigade ("Kvadrat") on a brief visit to local villagers. 1984. Southern Angola. Photo: V. Volodin (in the center)

★**29.** Chief Military Adviser in Angola (1982–1985) Col Gen Konstantin Kurochkin in FAPLA combat uniform. Upon his mission to Angola the Cuban leadership decorated him with the Order of Che Gevara (First Class). 1984. Photo: K. Kurochkin

★**30.** Mi-8 helicopter with a group of Angolan special operations troops moving to the area of combat landing. 1985. South-Eastern Angola. Photo: P. Suslov (veteran of Kaskad and Vympel KGB task force)

★32

★33

★31. A handshake over the map of Angola. Former Chief Military Adviser in Angola Col Gen Konstantin Kurochkin[16] meeting with the Cuban leader Fidel Castro Ruz. In the center – Minister of Defense Raúl Castro Ruz. 1987. Havana. Photo: Union of Angola Veterans archives

★32. Cuban military pilots Manuel Rojas Garcia (left) and Ramon Cáseda Aguilara captured by UNITA in Angola[17] were brought to the "opposition capital" of Jamba by force to take part in the UNITA military parade. November 11, 1987. Photo: UNITA special bulletin

★33. Soviet aviation specialists and Angolan helicopter pilots at an Angolan airfield. Mid-80ies. Photo: Union of Angola Veterans archives

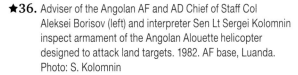

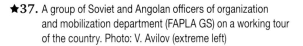

★34. A Soviet military adviser teaches rules of small arms handling to FAPLA fighters. 1989. Photo: V. Sagachko (left)

★35. A convoy of Angolan government troops came across a minefield. Mid-80ies. Photo: Union of Angola Veterans archives

★36. Adviser of the Angolan AF and AD Chief of Staff Col Aleksei Borisov (left) and interpreter Sen Lt Sergei Kolomnin inspect armament of the Angolan Alouette helicopter designed to attack land targets. 1982. AF base, Luanda. Photo: S. Kolomnin

★37. A group of Soviet and Angolan officers of organization and mobilization department (FAPLA GS) on a working tour of the country. Photo: V. Avilov (extreme left)

★38. Adviser to the Head of radio-technical department (Angolan Navy) Aleksandr Mokrenko speaking with Angolan officers. Photo: A. Korotkov

★39. A PLAN combat group secretly crosses the Angolan-Namibian border to conduct a rear area raid against the South African Defence Force in Namibia. Early 80ies. Photo: Union of Angola Veterans archives

★39

★41

★**40.** Angolan children enjoying the sun
and a new day without gunfire and air raids.
In the center – Soviet military interpreter
Lt Igor Bakush. 1989. Cuando Cubango
Province. Photo: I. Bakush

★**41.** Half-time of a football match. Left – captain
of the Angolan team President José Eduardo
dos Santos, center – captain of the Soviet
team Chief Military Adviser (1980–1982),
Hero of the Soviet Union Lt Gen Georgy
Petrovsky, right – interpreter-desk officer
of the CMA's Office Yury Klyukin.
Photo: Union of Angola Veterans archives

★42. Adviser of the Commander of the artillery
battalion (19th FAPLA Brigade) in Mulondo Maj
Vladimir Soldatenko with a tamed monkey.
1984, Mulondo. Photo: V. Soldatenko

★43. Sen Lt Vladimir Ovsyannikov assigned
to countersabotage watch crew on board
of *Leontiy Borisenko* diesel-powered ship and
its head radioman A. Timofeev. 1987, Luanda.
Photo: V. Ovsyannikov

★44. Soviet and Angolan officers of the 19th FAPLA
Infantry Brigade in on-site reconnaissance.
1983, Mulondo. Photo: O. Korgut

★45. Soviet officers against the famous
statue of Jesus Christ in Lubango. 1984.
Photo: V. Soldatenko (extreme right)

★46. BCh-3 combat department head
of *Stroiny* large anti-submarine ship
Sen Lt Maksim Ivanov (left) in preparation
to combat diving for demining the bottom
of Soviet ship *Kapitan Chirkov*[18].
1984, Port of Namibe. Photo: M. Ivanov

★47. Combat map of the Chief Military Adviser
in Angola. The map displays combat
situation as of August 23–27, 1981
in the Kunene Province[19]. Photo: Union
of Angola Veterans archives

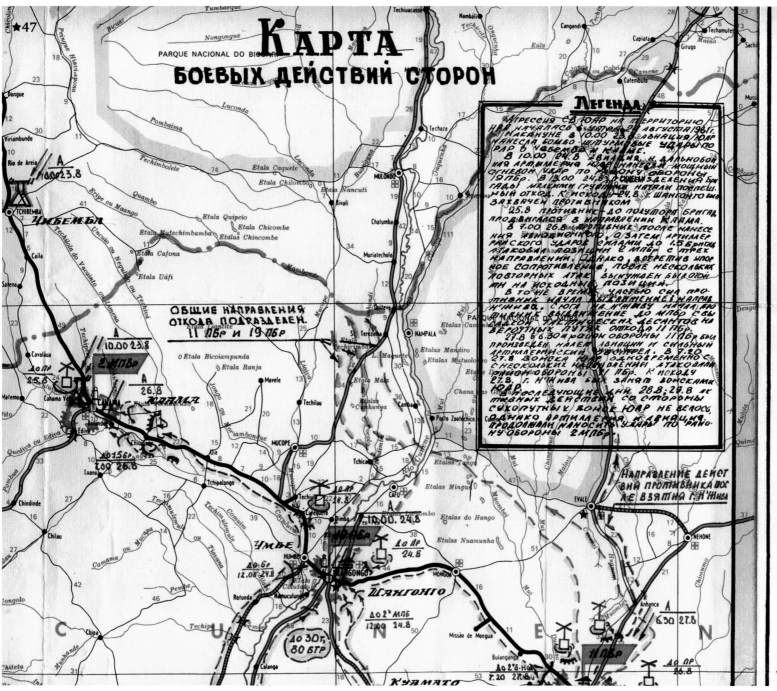

КАРТА БОЕВЫХ ДЕЙСТВИЙ СТОРОН

Parque Nacional do Bicoar

Легенда

Агрессия СВ ЮАР на территорию НРА началась 24 августа 1981 г. Накануне в 10.00 23.8 авиация ЮАР нанесла бомбо-штурмовые удары по РЛР в Чибемба и Каяма.

В 10.00 24.8 авиация и дальнобойная артиллерия ЮАР нанесла мощный огневой удар по 19 пбр. В 13.00 24.8 подразделения бригады мелкими группами начали поспешный отход. К исходу 24.8 Шангонго был захвачен противником.

25.8 противник до полутора бригад продвигался в направлении Каяма.

В 7.00 26.8 противник после нанесения авиационного и затем артиллерийского ударов силами до 1,5 бригад атаковал позиции 2 мпбр с трех направлений. Однако, встретив упорное сопротивление, после нескольких повторных атак вынужден был отойти на исходные позиции. В то же время часть сил противника начала выдвижение в направлении Н'Жива. Сюда началось выдвижение до мпбр с высадкой тактических десантов на вероятных путях отхода 11 пбр.

27.8 в 6.30 в район обороны 11 пбр был произведен налет авиации и сильный артиллерийский обстрел. В 7.20 27.8 войска ЮАР одновременно с нескольких направлений атаковали район обороны 11 пбр. К исходу 27.8 г. Н'Жива был занят войсками ЮАР.

В последующие дни 28.8; 29.8 активных действий со стороны сухопутных войск ЮАР не велось, однако артиллерия и авиация продолжали наносить удары по району обороны 2 мпбр.

Направление действий противника после взятия г. Н'Жива

Общие направления отхода подразделений 11 пбр и 19 пбр

31

---

23 августа 1981г.

10.00 — Авиация ЮАР нанесла бомбо-штурмовые удары по РЛР в г. Чибемба и в г. Каяма.

Выдвижение войск ЮАР (до двух бригад) в направлении Шангонго.

24 августа 1981г.

10.00 — Авиация и дальнобойная артиллерия нанесли мощный огневой удар по району обороны 19 пбр. (Уничт. КП, ТПУ, УС). Связь прервана

11.00 — Атака с неск. направл. Авиация воздейст. пост.

13.00 — Отход подразделений 19 пбр из Шангонго в северном направлений

к иск. 24.8.81 Шангонго захвачен войсками ЮАР

30.8.81 войска ЮАР ост. Шангон

25 августа 1981г.

В течение дня до 1,5 бригад выдвигались в направлении Шангонго Каяма

26 августа 1981г.

7.00 После артил. подготовки и нанесения авиационного удара, противник атаковал позиции 2 мпбр

После неоднокр. атак противник отошел в исх. положение

В течение 26.8.81 до двух усил. б-нов начали выдвижение в направл. Шангонго-Н'Жива, также до пбр с юга в напр. Намакунде-Н'Жива, высадив десант на вероятных путях отхода.

27 августа 1981г.

6.30 Артиллерийский обстрел и налет авиации

7.20 Противник атаковал

★48

★49

★50

★48. Military interpreter, author of the lyrics of the Angola Veterans Union's hymn Aleksandr Polivin, is choosing plotlines for the documentary about the international mission in Angola. 1989. Photo: A. Polivin

★49. A farewell to Soviet pilots of the An-12 aircraft crew[20], side number 11 747, CMA's air wing, shot down by a South African raiding force on November 25, 1985 in the vicinity of Menongue. 1985, Luanda. Photo: N. Shurygin

★50. A farewell to military interpreter of the 21st FAPLA Motorized Infantry Brigade Jr Lt Oleg Snitko killed in action on September 24. 1987 in the vicinity of Cuito Cuanavale. Among the escort of honor – military interpreters Sergei Antonov and Sergei Sinyakov. September 1987, Soviet military mission in Luanda. Photo: Union of Angola Veterans archives

★51. President of Angola José Eduardo dos Santos expresses gratitude to the Soviet crew of Mi-8 helicopter upon landing at destination shaking hands with flight technician Mikhail Sakharov. To the right – military pilot Sergei Golovchenko and crew commander Capt Yury Maevsky. May 1985, Southern Angola. Photo: M. Sakharov

★52

★**52.** In the area of combat operations.
Military interpreters in Angola (from left to right):
Aleksandr Fomin, Igor Sechin, Pavel Kamenets.
1985, Southern Angola. Photo: A. Fomin

★**53.** Military interpreter Igor Sechin
with his battlefield Angolan friend.
1986, Cuito Cuanavale. Photo: I. Sechin

★**54.** Missile battery commander
(*Admiral Yumashev* large anti-submarine
ship) Sen Lt Aleksandr Kononovich
with the employees of the Museum
of Angolan Armed Forces. 1984, Luanda,
Fortress Sao Miguel. Photo: A. Kononovich

★**55.** Personnel of the Angolan naval base
fall into line to welcome the Soviet military
delegation headed by the Deputy Chief
of Army and Navy Political Department[21]
Col Gen Viktor Nechayev. 1984. Luanda.
Photo: Union of Angola Veterans archives

★53

★54

★55

★57

★56. At the command post of government troops. Soviet military advisers examine a French APILAS AT rocket launcher captured from UNITA troops. Operation "Independência" (in preparation to operation "Zebra"). October-November 1989, South Eastern Angola. Photo: P. Zolotarev (holds the rocket launcher)

★57. Soviet military advisers of SWAPO in Angola (K. Satenov in front) and Namibian commanders of the 20th PLAN Brigade planning a new operation against UNITA troops. 1987, Andulo, Bié Province. Photo: I. Ignatovich

★58.Commemorative picture with an Angolan special task force after a successful operation. In the center – adviser of the Head of Special Operations Department of Angolan State Security Ministry, veteran of the KGB special task force Kaskad and Vympel Pyotr Suslov. 1987. Photo: P. Suslov

★59. Soviet civil specialist Mikhail Manayev with a tamed monkey. 1986. Photo: M. Manayev

★60. Soviet military advisers help in mastering an AGS-17 Plamya, Soviet automatic grenade launcher which has become operational in Angolan Army. 1982. Photo: O. Shashenkov (sitting, left)

★61. A picture of Soviet military specialist Aleksandr Malyarenko with Angolan FAPA[22] airman and DAA[23] soldier symbolizes the unity of Angolan Air Force and Air Defense. Malyarenko is dressed in Cuban "verde oliva" uniform habitually worn by Soviet advisers in the early years of cooperation. 1977. AF base, Luanda. Photo: A. Malyarenko

★61

★62. Training of the AGS-17 Plamya grenade launcher Angolan combat crew (18th FAPLA Air Assault Brigade). Soviet military specialist Vasily Stesyukov – center. 1985. Cuito, Bié Province. Photo: Union of Angola Veterans archives

★63. An Angolan soldier of the 19th FAPLA Infantry Brigade in ambush with a Soviet B-10 recoilless gun. 1987. Mulondo. Photo: O. Korgut

★64. Soviet officers assigned to the Angolan Navy make up a display about their service in Angola. Center – specialist in missile technology Capt 3rd rank Nikolai Sedov, right – instructor of the Naval training center Capt 2nd rank Gennady Kupriyanchik. 1986. Naval base, Luanda. Photo: A. Korotkov

★**65.** Last-minute preparations before combat. From left to right: adviser of the Commander of the 25th Infantry Brigade Lt Col Anatoly Kalyanov, adviser of the AD Chief of the 25th Infantry Brigade Lt Col Valery Sinyansky, interpreter Capt Igor Bokarev (sitting). 1988. Cuito Cuanavale. Photo: I. Bokarev

★**66.** Congratulations on the occasion of the International Women's Day to the wives of Soviet logistic support specialists (ships and aviation logistics of the Northern Fleet). 1988. Luanda. Photo: N. Melnikov

★**67.** Arrival and departure. A chance meeting of old friends at the airfield in Menongue. Aleksandr Polivin (left) and Vadim Sagachko on the ramp of an An-26 aircraft of the CMA performing a flight Luanda-Menongue-Luanda. May 1990. Photo: V. Sagachko

★68

★69

44

★70

★71

★72

★73

★**68.** Our advisers and specialists in Angola often lived in dugouts and tents. Author and cameraman of *We Couldn't Have Been There* documentary Aleksandr Polivin at location of unit lines of an Angolan brigade at Cuito Cuanavale. 1990. Photo: A. Polivin

★**69.** Capt Aleksandr Fomin before live-fire exercise. 1987. Southern Angola. Photo: A. Fomin

★**70.** A unique picture. Secret unloading of BM-21 "Grad"[24] multiple rocket launcher from An-22 aircraft (USSR military transport aviation division in the Congo, Brazzaville)[25]. November 1975

★**71.** A shot-down Mi-24 helicopter of the Angolan AF

★**72.** Command post of the 10th FAPLA Infantry Brigade. Soviet military advisers with a group of brigade officers. 1988, Cuando Cubango Province. Photo: A. Pobortsev (sitting, extreme left)

★**73.** Training exercise in mastering T-34 tank with PLAN fighters. Among Namibian soldiers – specialist in maintenance and repair of armor Sen Lt Andrei Mikhailichenko and military interpreter Lt Stanislav Sidorin. 1980, SWAPO Jamba Training Center, Lubango, Huila Province, Jamba. Photo: S. Sidorin

★74

★76

★75

★77

46

★78

★79

★74. Soviet advisers with the Angolan Navy at field firing with small arms. In front (with AKM assault rifle) – adviser of the Commander of missile boat division Capt 2nd rank Anatoly Sokolovsky. 1986. Luanda suburbs. Photo: A. Korotkov

★75. AF Commander of Angolan Air Defense Ciel da Conceição "Gato" (center) with staff officers and advisers after inspection of a Tu-95RTs reconnaissance plane at Luanda airfield. 1982. Photo: Union of Angola Veterans archives

★76. Adviser of the Commander of BM-14 multiple rocket launcher battery Capt Sergei Fyodorov (left) assigns a mission to the Angolan officer in dealing a blow on the enemy. 1987, Lucusse, 57th FAPLA Mechanized Infantry Brigade. Photo: S. Fyodorov

★77. Ceremonial replacement of Soviet color with the Angolan flag on the missile boat (205ER design) handed over to Angola. 1982. Naval base, Luanda. Photo: A. Bobovsky

★78. Soviet surveyors at the vista point of the Serra da Leba pass. 1980. Photo: N. Simakov (standing, right)

★79. Military interpreter cadet Sergei Kolomnin with an Angolan airfield guard in Namibe. 1977. Photo: S. Kolomnin

★80. Loading of BM-21 "Grad" multiple rocket launcher
on the deck of a large landing ship, 1171 design.
Angola coast waters. Photo: S. Remizov

★81. Military interpreter of the 21st FAPLA Infantry
Brigade Lt Mikhail Korol with Angolan children.
1985. Luacano, Moxico Province. Photo: M. Korol

★82. Adviser of the Chief of radio-technical department
of the Angolan Navy Aleksandr Mokrenko (in the center)
and military interpreter Igor Sechin speaking with
an Angolan officer on board an Angolan missile boat.
1985. Naval base, Luanda. Photo: A. Korotkov

★84

★85

★86

★83. BM-21 "Grad" rocket artillery battalion is ready to salvo
fire. 1983. N'dalatando. Photo: adviser of the Bn Cmdr
Lt Col Ye. Minyakovsky

★84. A view from the An-12 aircraft of the CMA's air wing.
Photo: Union of Angola Veterans archives

★85. The picture shows a live salvo of a BM-21 "Grad"
multiple rocket launcher delivered on the enemy.
Due to reconnaissance Soviet advisers managed to set up
an artillery attack on South African G-5 long-range howitzer
positions. 1987. Lomba River area. Photo: S. Mishchenko

★86. AML-90 armored vehicle of FNLA[26] troops destroyed
by the fire of FAPLA fighters in the battle of Quifangondo
on November 10, 1975. Quifangondo vicinity.
Photo: Union of Angola Veterans archives

★87. Soviet specialists and interpreters load ammunition belts
for KPVT heavy machine guns mounted on the turrets
of BTR-60PB APCs. 1987. Photo: A. Fomin (in front, standing)

★88. Adviser of the Commander of artillery battalion
of the 19th FAPLA Infantry Brigade Vladimir Soldatenko
writes a letter back home. 1984. Mulondo.
Photo: Union of Angola Veterans archives

★89. Crew of the Mi-8 Soviet helicopter of aerial mapping,
side number 22581, and a group of Soviet surveyors
with Angolan children. On June 9, 1981 in the course
of regular topographic research in Northern Angola
the helicopter was shot down by the ground troops,
all pilots and survey party killed in action[27].
1981. Photo: N. Simakov

★90. Training center at Malanje. Training of a reconnaissance
company of the newly shaped FAPLA brigade.
April, 1990. Photo: V. Sagachko

★90

★92

★93

★91. Naval base in Luanda. Torpedo and missile boats, mine sweepers and other Soviet-built ships which in the 80ies made the core of combat capabilities of the Angolan Navy[28] docked at the piers. Photo: Union of Angola Veterans archives

★92. Joint roll call of Soviet and Angolan naval mariners on the occasion of handing over of Soviet-built missile boats (205ER design) to the Angolan Navy. 1984. Naval base in Luanda. Photo: A. Sedov

★93. Adviser of the Fleet gunnery officer of the Angolan Navy Capt 1st rank Valentin Popov (in the center) among naval mariners on the navigation bridge of an Angolan combat ship. 1981. Photo: Union of Angola Veterans archives

★94

95

★96

★**94.** Military pilot of the 392ⁿᵈ Separate
Aviation Regiment of Long-range
Reconnaissance (Northern Fleet)
G. Simachev flies a Tu-95RTs airplane.
1979. Photo: Ye. Kalinin

★**95.** Crew of the Tu-95RTs reconnaissance
airplane at the logistics base in Luanda.
Building of the former Catholic English
School housing logistics personnel,
pilots and technicians can be seen
in the background. The slogan
in the Portuguese reads
"Long live Soviet-Angolan friendship".
1980. Photo: Ye. Kalinin

★**96.** Rolling of a Tu-95RTs reconnaissance
airplane to the apron in Luanda airport
after its landing. 1979. Photo: Ye. Kalinin

★**97.** Head of the group of Soviet military
specialists with SWAPO Col Nikolai Kurushkin
(left) on his tour of PLAN military posts
hands over his duties before departure
to the USSR. His successor, adviser
of the SWAPO Secretary for Defense,
head of the group of CMA with SWAPO
Col Boris Perebillo (right) with his wife.
1983. Photo: N. Kurushkin

★98

★100

★99

★101

★102

★98. Commanding officers of the Angolan Navy headed
by Admiral António da Carvalho "Toca" (third from the right)
with his Soviet adviser Capt 1st rank Ivan Kulinich
(extreme right). 1989. Naval base, Luanda.
Photo: Union of Angola Veterans archives

★99. Crew of a Soviet An-12 aircraft of the CMA's air wing
(side number 11747) from the 369th Regiment
of the USSR military transport aviation and ground
technicians before the last sortie in Angola.
From left to right: A. Kukuev, S. Grishenkov, S. Lukyanov,
Lishkunov, A. Nikitin, V. Shibanov, V. Osadchuk, V. Pshenyuk.
1985. Luanda airport. Photo: N. Shurygin

★100. An address of the adviser of the PLAN ChofS
Col Aleksandr Veres to SWAPO fighters in Angola.
Extreme right, bespectacled – SWAPO army ChofS
Charles Namolo "Ho Chi Minh". 1987. Xangongo-Onjiva area.
Photo: I. Ignatovich (standing second from the right)

★101. Wives of Soviet military advisers and specialists in Angola
often visited the firing range with their husbands to practice
small arms application for self-defense purposes.
1987. Negage. Photo: V. Kukk

★102. A group of Angolan students of Soviet military academies
headed by João Manuel Lourenço (in 1978–1982 – student
of Military-Political Academy named after V.I. Lenin,
standing in the center) go sightseeing in Leningrad
(now – St. Petersburg). In 2017 J.M. Lourenço was elected
President of the Republic of Angola. 1981. Photo: I. Korolev

★104

★105

★103. Soviet specialists with SWAPO in Angola with a PLAN
female fighter. Second from the right – head of the group
of Soviet military specialists Col Nikolai Kurushkin.
1982. Lubango, Huila Province. Photo: N. Kurushkin

★104. Head of the group of Soviet military specialists with SWAPO
in Angola Col Nikolai Kurushkin and PLAN Commander,
SWAPO Secretary for Defense Peter Nanyemba[29].
1982. Photo: N. Kurushkin

★105. SWAPO adviser in Angola Vladimir Stryukov
with the family of a PLAN fighter and his friends.
1985. Lubango, Huila Province. Photo: V. Stryukov

61

★106. Luanda seaport – an ocean gateway of the country.
Upon declaration of Angola's independence in the framework
of operation "Carlota"[30] in November–December 1975
the seaport received ships with internationalist fighters
from Cuba and large cargo carriers from the USSR
with arms and military hardware. Supported
by the assistance in 1975–1976 the MPLA managed
to repel the armed aggression of SA and Zairean Armies.

★107. Angolan fishing port of Boa Vista. In the 80ies in the settlement
of Cacuaco near Luanda the Soviet Ministry of Fisheries
helped to establish and successfully operate a training
facility where Soviet teachers trained Angolan specialists
for national fishing fleet.

★108. Unloading of the fish catch in Angolan port. In the 70ies
the USSR handed over six fishing motorboats (MRTK type)
without compensation which regularly supplied the capital's
inhabitants with fresh fish. Besides, in the framework
of inter-government agreement the Soviet fleet fishing
in the Angolan economic zone supplied dozens of thousand
tons of fish products to the local population as compensation
for fishing rights

★109. A Soviet instructor of the Industrial college in Huambo
teaches an Angolan student to operate a turning lathe.
1986. Photo: V. Perventsev

★110. A supervising foreman from the USSR monitors
the work of Angolan college students.
1986. Huambo. Photo: V. Perventsev

★111. Unloading of Soviet Kamaz trucks in the Angolan seaport. 1985. Luanda.

★112. An Angolan car mechanic trained by Soviet instructors repairs motor vehicles supplied by the Soviet Union. 1986. Photo: V. Perventsev

★113. A Soviet supervising foreman helps Angolan students in mastering new equipment. 1985. Photo: V. Perventsev

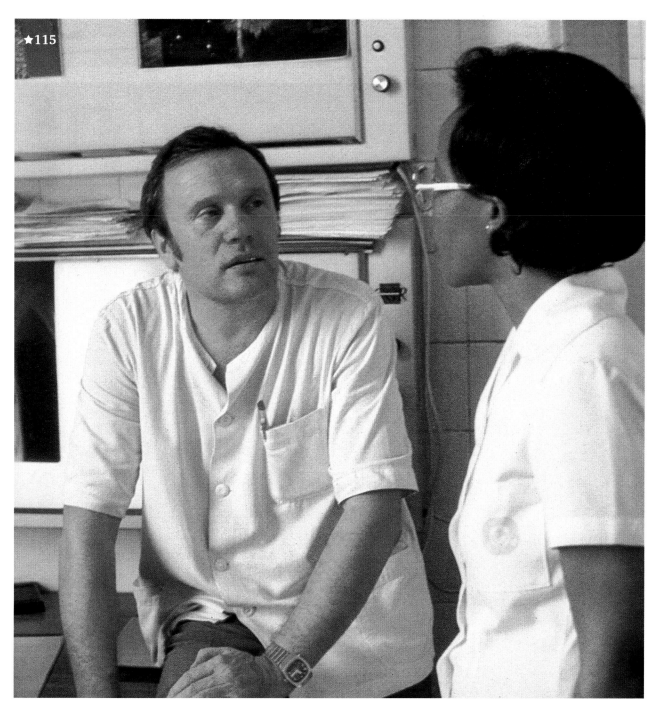

★115

★**114.** Acceptance of Soviet agricultural
equipment delivered to Angola.
1986. Photo: V. Perventsev

★**115.** In the 80ies Soviet medical doctors rendered
vast assistance to Angola in the development
of national public health care.
1986. Photo: V. Perventsev

A delegation of the Union of Angola Veterans in the Moscow Mayor's Office. The Memorial Day of the Russians who carried out their service duty beyond national borders. February 15, 2017

We Live with the Present and Confidently Look into the Future

The Russian Union of Angola Veterans actively works in the framework of the RF Law "On Public Associations". Before all, the Union is designed to support internationalist and patriotic upbringing of Russian citizens, promote development of public, cultural, economic and military ties with the Republic of Angola, as well as to preserve the true story of internationalist assistance to Angola in 1975–1992 rendered by Russian and former USSR citizens to be retold to future generations. Those efforts of the Union are manifold. Among them are: organization of public exhibitions and conferences, commemorative and memorial events, meetings of the veterans with Russian youth, Angolan students and cadets studying in Russian institutions, campaign-motor rallies. The Union also shapes and equips museums and displays, undertakes publications in the media, publication and distribution at home and abroad of books, brochures, booklets and documentaries showing how Russians and former Soviet citizens accomplished their internationalist and service duty in Angola in 1975–1992. Still another component is celebration of the annual Day of Angola Veterans (November 16), decoration of the veterans with Union's medals and other events.

One of the dynamic guidelines of the Russian Union of Angola Veterans are the activities in the framework of public (or people's) diplomacy. As it is known, before all the term implies active unofficial contacts of common people and public organizations. Such contacts contribute to the improvement of relations, mutually beneficial cooperation, better understanding of culture, history, traditions and specific features of everyday life of different countries. The Union of Angola Veterans has a vast capability to perform this job based on wide experience of its members to socialize with Angolans acquired at the time of their work in the country.

Members of the Union united into Moscow (central) and seventeen regional organizations (Altai Territory, Vologda Region, Vladivostok, Kaliningrad, Kirov Region, City of Kolomna, St. Petersburg, Leningrad and Novosibirsk Regions, Republic of Mordovia, Tver, Tula, Republic of Crimea and the City of Sevastopol, Saratov, Syzran and Yaroslavl Region) actively meet with Angolan students and cadets studying in

Russia, Angolan delegations visiting our country, and conduct meetings when visiting Angola and Cuba.

Russian Foreign Minister S. Lavrov highly praised the contribution of Union members into public diplomacy. In his address to the readers of the book (*We Carrieed Out Our Duty. Angola: 1975–1992*) published by the Union he noted: "A special role in building trust and mutual understanding between the two nations belong to public diplomacy. A significant contribution into joint efforts is made by the Russian Union of Angola Veterans which upholds close contacts with partner organizations. It is gratifying to know that our Angolan and Cuban friends take part in its activities".

Due to the dynamics of the Union on the path of people's diplomacy it tangibly succeeded in perpetuation of the memory of Russian and Soviet citizens and their exploits in Angola. As a result of lengthy consultations and talks with Angolan officials, numerous friendly meetings and discussions with our Angolan comrades-in-arms and war veterans we managed to reach an agreement on erecting a monument. On March 5, 2018 the official opening ceremony of the memorial stone was held in the Angolan capital on the premises of the Russian Embassy school. The monument carries a plaque with the inscription in Russian and Portuguese: "In commemoration of those who fought for independent Angola. To the Russians who carried out their internationalist duty".

Photographs presented in the second part of the album show this milestone event as well as dozens of other events in the life of the Russian Union of Angola Veterans, describe its active and fruitful efforts, and purposeful onward movement.

The strategic mission of the Russian Union of Angola Veterans is to preserve, protect and circulate the live MEMORY of the past based on true and actual knowledge of history, to help understand the importance and sustainability of cooperation with the country which became free and independent with the help of the USSR and Russia.

★116. A monument in the memory of Quifangondo defenders[31]. Angola

★117. Russian President Vladimir Putin and President
of the Republic of Angola João Manuel Gonçalves Lourenço
after official talks in the Kremlin. April, 2019. Moscow

★118. Embankment in the Angolan capital Luanda. Today's view

★**119.** During his visit to Cuba Russian Prime-Minister Dmitry Medvedev presents the Badge of the Honorary Member of Angola Veterans Union and the medal "For Rendering International Assistance to Angola" to Raúl Castro Ruz. In the center – Aleksandr Fomin. February, 2013. Havana.
Photo: Union of Angola Veterans archives

★**120.** The memorial stone in Luanda carries a plaque which reads in Russian and Portuguese: "In commemoration of those who fought for independent Angola. To the Russians who carried out their internationalist duty". The monument was erected on the initiative of the Union of Angola Veterans on March 5, 2018

★**121.** The opening ceremony attended by the Angolan Ministers of Foreign Affairs and Defense, Ambassadors of Russia, Cuba, South Africa and Namibia was headed by the Russian Foreign Minister S. Lavrov. March 5, 2018.
Photo: Union of Angola Veterans archives

★**122.** The opening ceremony of the memorial in Luanda. March 5, 2018

★**123.** A handshake of S. V. Lavrov and Angolan Minister of Defense Salviano Sequeira "Kianda". March 5, 2018. Opening ceremony of the memorial in Luanda

★**124.** Russian veterans of Angola laying flowers to the memorial stone in Luanda. 2018

★125

★128

★126

★127

★125. Honored guest from Angola João Manuel Gonçalves Lourenço on a visit to the office and museum of the Union of Angola Veterans in Moscow. August 3, 2015. Photo: A. Kalmykov

★126. Angola and Mozambique veteran Vladimir Gruzdev (second from the left) is awarded with the Badge of the Honorary Member of Union of Angola Veterans. 2011. RF State Duma. Photo: Union of Angola Veterans archives

★127. Members of the Union's office in the Republic of Crimea meet with Angolan cadets of the Higher Naval School named after P. Nakhimov. 2018. Sevastopol. Photo: A. Karyakin

★128. Russian veterans of Angola attend the research-to-practice conference devoted to the 20th anniversary of the Cuito Cuanavale battle. April 19, 2018. Institute for African Studies of the RAS. Moscow. Photo: Union of Angola Veterans archives

★129

★131

★130

★132

★**129.** On his official visit to Moscow João Manuel Gonçalves Lourenço visits the museum of the Union of Angola Veterans in Moscow. August 3, 2015. Photo: A. Kalmykov

★**130.** Angola veterans Sergei Grigoryev, Ilya Khakhankin and Sergei Remizov at the opening ceremony of the memorial stone of the Grove of Commemoration of KIA in local conflicts[32]. 2018. Kolomna. Photo: A. Kalmykov

★**131.** Angola veterans Alekrsandr Kononovich, Viktor Medvedev and Albert Shinkarev at the ceremonial event in the Moscow Mayor's Office devoted to the 10th anniversary of the foundation of "Officers of Russia" public organization. June 14, 2017. Photo: S. Remizov

★**132.** Head of the Union's office in Syzran Col (Ret.) Valery Kukk meets with Angolan students of the Russian AF training center[33]. 2018. Syzran. Photo: V. Kukk

★**133.** Angolan Minister for Veterans of War and Labor João Ernesto dos Santos "Liberdade"[34] makes an entry into the Book of Honorary Visitors of the Angola Veterans museum. April 15, 2018. Moscow. Photo: S. Balakleyev

★133

81

★135

★138

★136

★139

★137

★140

★**134.** Vadim Sagachko and Sergei Kolomnin present to General Simão Carlitos Wala a renovated and enlarged photograph capturing him with his fighters who distinguished themselves in the "Kissonde" operation[35]. April 5, 2019. Russian Military Academy of the General Staff[36]. Photo: S. Balakleyev

★**135.** Head of the Angola Veterans' Union office in the Kaliningrad Region Igor Bukhalin at the monument to KIA in local wars. 2018. Kaliningrad. Photo: I. Bukhalin

★**136.** Veteran airmen, members of the Union's office in Dzhankoy, at the monument to the pilots of the 369th Regiment of Transport Aviation KIA in Angola. November 25. 2016. Dzhankoy, Crimea. Photo: N. Shurygin (left)

★**137.** Coordinator of the section of civil specialists-members of the Union Svetlana Polyakova with students of the Krasnodar Presidential cadet school at the exhibition "Military interpreters serving their Motherland". June 6, 2017. Moscow. Photo: Ye. Loginov

★**138.** Head of the Union office in Syzran Valery Kukk holds a presentation of the book *We Have Carried Out Our Duty. Angola 1975–1992*. 2016. Photo: V. Kukk

★**139.** Members of the Union's office in the Novosibirsk Region meet with the veterans of local wars in the museum of secondary school # 1 of Chulymsk District. February 15, 2018. Photo: S. Likhosherstov (second, right)

★**140.** Veterans of Angola and local wars in a campaign trip across the Crimea. 2018. Photo: A. Karyakin

★**141.** General José Santos Paulino, student of the RF Armed Forces
General Staff Academy, at the presentation of Sergei Kolomnin's
book *We Have Carried Out Our Duty. Angola: 1975 – 1992*, May
2016. Photo: S. Balakleyev

★**142.** Union members in the Crimea and Sevastopol with Angolan
students of P. Nakhimov Higher Naval School at the Monument
to the Sunken Ships, 2018. Sevastopol, Crimea.
Photo: A. Bobkovsky (centre, standing)

★143

★144

★**143.** Capt 2nd rank I. Bukhalin, head of the Kaliningrad Region
Union Office and Angola veteran Capt 1st rank I. Ushakov
with Angolan graduates of the F. Ushakov Baltic Naval Institute.
2019. Photo: I. Bukhalin

★**144.** Angolan naval mariners at the Angola Navy Day parade, July 10,
2018. Luanda. Photo: M. Styozhka

★**145.** Vadim Sagachko, head of the Angola Veterans Union,
receives a memorable gift from the Commander
of the Angolan Navy Fransisco José. The opening ceremony
of the photo exhibition "USSR (Russia's) Assistance
in Creating Angola's Navy (1975–1992)", July 4, 2017.
Union of Angola Veterans Museum. Photo: S. Balakleyev

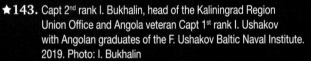

★145

★**146.** Pilots of 392[37] Separate Long-Range Reconnaissance Aviation Regiment (ODRAP) at the Fedotovo airfield[37]. 2011. Photo: E. Kalinin

★**147.** Crimean veterans of Angola with Angolan students of the P. Nakhimov Higher Naval School, Sevastopol. Photo: A. Karyakin (centre, standing)

★**148.** Angola veterans Daniyal Gukov, Kamil Mollayev, Natalya Volkova and Vladimir Volkov at the celebration of the 15th anniversary of the Union. November 16, 2019. Moscow. Photo: S. Balakleyev

★**149.** Vladimir Volkov hands over the book *We Have Carried Out Our Duty. Angola: 1975–1992* to the employees of the Ulyanovsk Memorial Museum. 2016. Photo: V. Volkov

★**150.** Angola veterans Mikhail Fedosyuk and Vladimir Averkin at the celebration of the 15th anniversary of the Union. November 16, 2019. Moscow. Photo: S. Balakleyev

★**151.** Union of Angola Veterans' awards presented to the Cuban leader Fidel Castro[38]. February 2013, Havana

★149

★150

★151

★152

★**152.** Members of the Union of Angola Veterans delegation Aleksei Pobortsev and Igor Bakush (left, centre) with Russian military advisers at the memorial stone set up in commemoration of Soviet and Russian internationalists who did their international duty in Angola. March 2018. Luanda. Photo: S. Kolomnin

★**153.** Aleksei Pobortsev, chief of the NTV Company special projects department, Angola veteran, hands over a disk with the copy of his film Angola: *War that Never Was* to General Salviano Sequeira "Kianda" Angola's Defense Minister. March 2018. Luanda. Photo: A. Pobortsev

★154.

★154. Former Commander of the 392th Military Transport Aviation Regiment[39] Col (Ret.) A. Lobanov hands over to Nikolai Shurygin, head of the Dzhankoy Union Office (Crimea) a valuable gift and certificate of merit "For Active Commemoration Work". May 5, 2018. Dzhankoy. Photo: F. Shakirov

★155. Meeting Angolan students of Moscow's military academies in the residence of the Angola Veterans Union. Left to right: Tenghiz Chikobava, Rear-Admiral Alberto Victor Fernando, Lt Gen Joao da Cruz Fonseca, Vadim Sagachko. May 2016. Photo: A. Kalmykov

★156. General of the Army, Chief of Russia's Armed Forces General Staff Valery Gerasimov hands over a diploma and gold medal to the graduate of the RF General Staff Military Academy, honorary member of the Angola Veterans Union Lt Gen Simao Carlitos Wala. June 20, 2019. Moscow. Photo: S. Balakleyev

★155.

★156

Памяти погибших в Анголе
25 ноября 1985 г.
советских военных летчиков
и советников:

СЕРГЕЯ ЛУКЬЯНОВА, АЛЕКСЕЯ НИКИТИНА,
ВЛАДИМИРА ЖУРКИНА, ВИКТОРА ОСАДЧУКА,
СЕРГЕЯ ГРИЩЕНКОВА, ВЛАДИМИРА ШИБАНОВА,
ВИТАЛИЯ ПШЕНЮКА, СЕРГЕЯ ШОЛМОВА,
АЛЕКСАНДРА МАРТЫНОВА,
ЕВГЕНИЯ КАНДИДАТОВА,
МИХАИЛА ЖЕРНОСЕКА, АНАТОЛИЯ ПЕРЕВЁРТОВА

★158

★159

★157. On September 25, 2015 in Angola near the town of Menongue at the site of the crash of the USSR military transport plane An-12, side number 11747, was installed a monument to the crew and Soviet military advisers on board killed in the crash. In the photo Aleksei Pobortsev and Yelena Nikitina, widow of the second in command Aleksei Nikitin. Photo: A. Stvolin

★158. Vadim Sagachko hands over the Union's public medal "For Internationalist Assistance to Angola" to a Cuban veteran-internationalist. Far right Nikolai Rybchuk, Union's representative in Angola. 2015. Luanda. Photo: S. Kolomnin

★159. Members of the Union's Crimean office with Angolan students of the P. Nakhimov Higher Naval School. 2018. Sevastopol. Photo: A. Karyakin (centre, with a banner)

★**160.** Traditional meeting of Angola veterans at the celebration of the Victory Day at the Gorky Central Park. May 9, 2017. Moscow. Photo: S. Balakleyev

★**161.** Member of the Union, Hero of Russia, Merited Test Pilot of the Russian Federation Ruben Esayan presents to the Rector of the Temple of Military Memory of the Valaam Monastery[40] Hieromonk David, the book *We Have Carried Out Our Duty. Angola: 1975–1992.* 2016. Valaam. Photo: S. Polyakova

★**162.** Members of the Saratov Union office led by its head Valentin Veranovsky at the Memorial "To the Compatriots Fallen in Local Wars". 2018. Saratov, Park Pobedy. Photo: A. Buchnev

★**163.** Memorial "To the Compatriots Fallen in Local Wars". 2018. Saratov, Park Pobedy. Photo: A. Buchnev

★**164.** Members of the Vologda Union office (left to right): Valery Tsipilev, Yevgeny Kalinin and Oleg Oleinikov. 2012. Fedotovo airfield, Vologda Region

★**165.** The RF Flag Ceremony. Day of remembrance for Russians who performed their official duty outside their Fatherland. 2018. Moscow Mayor's Office. Photo: S. Balakleyev

★**166.** Svetlana Polyakova, coordinator of the division of civilian specialists-members of the Union at the photo exhibition of the Union "Angola. An important milestone". November 2015. Photo: A. Kalmykov

★**167.** Head of the Yaroslavl Union office Vladimir Blinov tells Angolan students of the Yaroslavl Higher Anti-Aircraft Defense Military School about the military history of the college graduates. 2018. Yaroslavl. Photo: V. Blinov

★**168.** Members of the Samara Region Union office and Angolan students took part in the inauguration ceremony of the monument to Mig-15 plane in the Syzran Higher Military Pilots Aviation School[41]. The right to unveil the monument was granted to the college graduate Air Force Maj Gen (Ret.), Union member Vladimir Feoktistov who was adviser of the Angolan Air Force and Anti-Aircraft Defense Commander in 1987–1990. July 30, 2019. Syzran. Photo: V. Kukk

★166

★167

★168

★169

★**169.** Aleksei Kalmykov, head of the Union's research party.
2019. Photo: S. Balakleyev

★**170.** Vladimir Kazimirov, Ambassador to Angola in 1987–1990,
greets Angola veterans – marines Ivan Kisilev
and Nikolai Almakov. November 16, 2019.
Moscow. Photo: S. Balakleyev

★**171.** Angolan cadets from P. Nakhimov Higher Naval School
on an excursion. 2018. Sevastopol. Photo: B. Bobkovsky

★**172.** Angola veteran Nikolai Tulov with his wife and daughter
at the celebration of the 15th anniversary of the Union.
November 16, 2019. Moscow. Photo: S. Balakleyev

★**173.** Sergei Remizov presents the head of the Mordovia office
Sergei Durdayev with the medal "For Combat Service
in the Atlantic". 2018. Photo: A. Kalmykov

★**174.** Valery Kukk presents Angolan cadets with memorial medals
"40 Years Together", February 15, 2018. Photo: V. Kukk

★170

★171

★173

★172

★174

Саратовское ВВА

101

★176

★178

★177

★**175.** Meeting of the members of the Syzran office of the Angola Veterans Union with Russian and Angolan cadets of the Military Educational and Scientific Centre at the Zhukovsky and Gagarin Air Force Academy. 2018. Photo: V. Kukk

★**176.** During the visit of the South African Defence Force veterans to the Moscow museum of the Union the head of the delegation Gen Roland de Vries was presented with the book *Military Chronicle of Russia in Pictures. 1850–2000* published with the assistance of the Union of Angola Veterans. From left to right: Barry Fowler[42], Igor Ignatovich, R. de Vries, Vadim Sagachko. June 2014. Moscow. Photo: A. Kalmykov

★**177.** Union of Angola Veterans Museum in Moscow. Fragment of the exposition. 2019. Photo: S. Balakleyev

★**178.** Sergei Kolomnin presents Douw Steyn, the former commander of the 4th South African Defence Force Commando Unit (4 Recce), with the Russian version of the magazine *Soldier of Fortune* with his article on secret operations of Recces combat swimmers in Angola. July 12, 2016. Museum of Union of Angola Veterans, Moscow[43]. Photo: M. Gladkov

★179

★180

★179. Laying floral tributes to the monument
of the pilots of the 369th Air Force Military
Transport Aviation Regiment who fulfilled
their internationalist duty in Angola.
2018. Dzhankoy, Crimea.
Photo: N. Shurygin

★180. Members of the Union Leningrad Regional
office Ilyas Norov (head of the office, left)
and Sergei Pavlov at the monument
"To Fighter-Internationalist".
February 15, 2019. Gatchina.
Photo: I. Norov

★181. Head of the Kolomna Union office
inaugurates a memorial stone in the
"Grove of Remembrance for the Fallen
in Local Conflicts" set out by him.
August 2, 2019. Kolomna.
Photo: A. Kalmykov

★182. Visit of the Namibian Republic delegation
headed by General Ndatipo to the Union's
residence in Moscow. Igor Ignatovich,
head of the Union's Namibian division,
shows to the guests a color brochure
*USSR and SWAPO: Secret Mission
in Angola*, published by the Union,
June 26, 2017. Photo: S. Balakleyev

★183. Veterans of the Union's Kaliningrad
office and relatives at the tomb
of Lt Col Yevgeny Kireyev and his wife
Lidia who were killed on August 27, 1981
in Angola in a battle with South African
troops. February 15, 2019. Kaliningrad
Municipal Cemetery. Photo: I. Bukhalin

★181

★182

★183

★184

★186

★185

★184. Former head of the group of Soviet specialists at the African National Congress (ANC)[44] in Angola Capt 1st rank Vyacheslav Shiriayev[45], best known among the ANC fighters under the combat name "Comrade Ivan", and António José Mateus, Press-Attaché of the Angolan Embassy in RF at the opening of the Union's photo exhibition "We Could Not Have Been There". June 2009. Photo: S. Balakleyev

★185. Angola veterans headed by Marine Lt Col Viktor Nadyozhin (Ret.) (centre) at the presentation of Sergei Kolomnin's book *We Have Carried Out Our Duty. Angola: 1975–1992*. 2016. Vladivostok. Photo: V. Nadyozhin

★186. Angola's President João Lourenço welcomes members of the Union's delegation Nikolai Rybchuk and Andrei Tokarev (centre) who made a report in Luanda on the support of the USSR and Russia to the Angolan people[46]. December 5, 2019. Photo: Angola's President press service

★187. A copy of the new film by A. Pobortsev *Two Wars* was ceremoniously handed over to the delegation of Angolan students of the General Staff Academy and Frunze Military Academy. The delegation was headed by the leader of the group of students from Angola in Russia Lt Gen Dinis Segunda Lucamare (centre). May 2016. Moscow. Photo: S. Balakleyev

★188

★190

★189

★191

★188. The Union's delegation at the celebration of the War Veterans Day at Poklonnaya Gora. July 1, 2019. Photo: S. Remizov

★189. Union members from the Crimea hand over the Union's books to the veterans' organization. December 4, 2018. Photo: A. Bashkardin

★190. Sergei Grigoriyev is awarded for active support of the Union of Angola Veterans[47]. November 16, 2019. Photo: S. Balakleyev

★191. V. Sagachko and. V. Shalnev talk to the Military Attaché of Mozambique in Russia Antonio de Zasa. The Union's 15th anniversary. November 16, 2019. Photo: S. Balakleyev

★192. A group of organizers and guests of the photo exhibition "Military Translators in Service of the Fatherland". June 2017. Photo: A. Kalmykov

★193. Angola veterans Igor Gorbunov and Vladimir Sukach at the Union's exhibition "Angola. An important milestone."

★192

★193

★194

★195

★196

★197

★**194.** Veterans of the Altai Territory Union's office after having been decorated with the medal "For Internationalist Assistance to Angola". Second right – Head of the Union's office in the Altai Territory Boris Kharitonov. November 16, 2018.
Photo: Angola Veterans Union archives

★**195.** Presentation of medals "For Internationalist Assistance to Angola" to veterans of the Leningrad Region. Far left – the head of the Union's office in the Region Iliyas Norov. 2018. Gatchina. Photo: I. Norov

★**196.** Lt Gen of Angola's Armed Forces Amilcar Devid Etossi, student of the General Staff Academy of RF Armed Forces at the presentation of the new film about Angola by A. Pobortsev *Two Wars*. May 2016. Residence of the Union of Angola Veterans, Moscow.
Photo: A. Kalmykov

★**197.** Angola veterans from all over Russia got together at the celebration of the 15th anniversary of the Union. The event was held under the slogan: "Remember the Past, Live in the Present, Look with Confidence into the Future". From left to right: Viktor Shalnov, Sergei Solomakha, Andrei Chezhidov. November 16, 2019. Moscow.
Photo: S. Balakleyev

★199

★200

★**198.** Vadim Sagachko presents to Valery Bitayev, fighter-internationalist, participant of the Cuito Cuanavale Battle, member of the Angola Veterans Union, the medal "For Internationalist Assistance to Angola". May 9, 2016.
Photo: Union of Angola Veterans archives

★**199.** Chief organizer of the jubilee party in honor of the 15th anniversary of the Union of Angola Veterans, fighter-internationalist Mikhail Styozhka and Rear Admiral Vladimir Dobroskochenko, Angola veteran, former commander of the 7th Operative Squadron. November 16, 2019.
Photo: S. Balakleyev

★**200.** Commander of Angola's Air Force Lt Gen Francisco Afonso "Hanga" hands over to Alexander Cherkassky, representative of the Union in Angola, a memorial badge of Angola's Air Force for the Union's museum in Moscow. 2018. Luanda.
Photo: A. Cherkassky

★**201.** Performance of the Russian Folk Ensemble "Grenada" under Tatiana Vladimirskaya at the festive celebration of the 15th anniversary of the Union of Angola Veterans. November 16, 2019. "Borodino-Hall" Hotel concert hall, Moscow. Photo: S. Balakleyev

★202

★203

★**202.** Russian pilot Kamil Mollayev, Angola's veteran, holder of the Order of Peoples' Friendship, who was captured by the UNITA and spent two years[48] in captivity (right) after having received the medal "For Internationalist Assistance to Angola" and the book *Russian Special Forces in Africa* written by Sergei Kolomnin, deputy-chairman of the Union. January 2012. Residence of the Union in Moscow. Photo: A. Kalmykov

★**203.** A group of Angola veterans from Transdniestria commemorates the Remembrance Day for the Russians who did their combat duty outside the Fatherland. February 15, 2018. Tiraspol. Photo: S. Fyodorov

★**204.** Russian veterans of Angola and members of the diplomatic corps in Luanda laying floral tributes to the memorial stone "In commemoration of those who fought for independent Angola. To the Russians who Carried Out their internationalist duty". The monument was set up on the initiative of the Union of Angola Veterans on March 5, 2018. Luanda. Photo: RF Embassy in Luanda

★**205.** Military delegation from Angola led by the Commander of the Angolan Navy Admiral Francisco Jose at the ceremony of opening the photo exhibition "Assistance of the USSR (Russia) in creating the Angolan Navy (1975–1992)". July 4, 2017. Union of Angola Veterans Museum. Photo: S. Balakleyev

★204

Помощь СССР (России) в создании военно-морского флота Анголы (1975-1992)

★205

★207

★208

★**206.** Angolan students of the P. Nakhimov Higher Naval School in Sevastopol examine military equipment in the Russian Black Sea Navy Museum. Crimea. Photo: A. Bobkovsky

★**207.** Russian and Angolan veterans at the celebration of 30 years of victory in the battle for Cuito Cuanavale in Angola. From left to right: Chairman of the Forum of Cuito Cuanavale fighters Lt Gen Fernando Mateus , Nikolai Rybchuk, Commander-in-Chief of Angola's Air Force Col Gen Francisco Afonso "Hanga", Sergei Kolomnin. March 2018. Photo: S. Scripnik

★**208.** Head of the Union's Vologda Region office Sergei Kononov (left) with activists of the Union Yevgeny Kalinin and Sergei Frolov. November 16, 2019. Moscow. Photo: S. Balakleyev

★210

★**209.** Presentation of Union member Yevgeny Kalinin's
book *Independent Long-Range Reconnaissance*[49]
to Commander-in Chief Col Gen of Angola's Air Force
Francisco Afonso "Hanga". In particular, the book
describes the work of Tu-95RTs reconnaissance planes
from the Luanda airfield in the 60–70ies of the 20th century.
2015. Luanda. Photo: A. Stvolin

★**210.** Vadim Sagachko presents to the South African
internationalist, former fighter of uMkhonto we Sizwe[50],
and currently South Africa's Ambassador to Luanda
the medal "For Internationalist Assistance to Angola".
2018. Luanda. Photo: S. Kolomnin

★**211.** Deputy head of the Union's Kaliningrad office
Capt 2nd rank (Ret.) Mikhail Puzik with the banner
of the Angola Veterans Union. November 16, 2019.
Celebration of the Union's 15th anniversary.
Photo: S. Balaklevev

★211

СОЮЗ ВЕТ

121

★212

★213

★**212.** Union's delegation hands over a gift to the Angola's Air Force History Museum to João Manuel Lourenço. 2015. Luanda. Photo: S. Kolomnin

★**213.** Union's delegation at the celebration of the 30th anniversary of victory in the battle for Cuito Cuanavale. 2018. Cuito Cuanavale. Photo: A. Stvolin

★**214.** I. Sechin, Vice-Premier of the RF government, tours the exhibition "*We Could Not Have Been There*". 2009. Moscow. Photo: Angola Veterans Union

★**215.** The Angolan delegation at the opening of the Union's exhibition *Was Not Angola's Land Red with Russian Blood?* 2006. Moscow. Photo: S. Kolomnin

★**216.** V. Sagachko with the Angolan security service for the Union's delegation before visiting the A. Neto Mausoleum in Luanda. 2015. Photo: S. Kolomnin

★**217.** A. Pobortsev hands over copies of his films about Angola to the veteran from Kazakhstan K. Satenov. 2018. Kazakhstan. Photo: A. Stvolin

★214

★216

★215

★217

★218. Leader of the Forum of fighters at Cuito Cuanavale
Lt Gen Antonio Valeriano signs the Book of Honorary
Visitors of the Angola Veterans Union's museum in Moscow
after receiving the medal "30 Years of Victory in the Battle
for Cuito Cuanavale". 2018. Photo: S. Balakleyev

★219. Head of the Syzran Union office Col (Ret.) Valery Kukk
and Angola veteran Maj (Ret.) Aleksandr Sidorov
at the celebration of the 15th anniversary
of the Union of Angola Veterans in Moscow.
November 16, 2019. Photo: S. Balakleyev

★220. Aleksandr Fomin, Director of Russia's Service
for Military and Technical Cooperation, Angola
veteran (on the right) presents Angola's President
José Eduardo dos Santos a badge of the honorary
member of the Union of Angola Veterans. October 2013.
Photo: Angolan President's protocol service

★221

★222

★223

★**221.** Former ambassador to Angola Victor Kazimirov (second left) always has a story to tell to his fellow comrades about his Angolan ambassadorship. Angola Veterans Day. November 16, 2013. Moscow. Photo: A. Kalmykov

★**222.** Angola veterans Capt 2nd rank Vladimir Ovsyannikov (right) and WO Boris Barvinok recall their service in Angola. 2015. Union's Museum in Moscow. Photo: A Kalmykov

★**223.** Angola veterans from Saratov at the opening of the exhibition "Saratov Pages of "Cold War". Angola" (from left to right): Aleksandr Rydanov, Aleksandr Buchnev, Tatyana Khudoyerko[51], Alexei Khudoyerko. November 2013. Saratov, Museum of Military Glory. Photo: A. Buchnev

★**224.** Angola's Minister for War and Labor Veterans Affairs João E. dos Santos "Liberdade" tours the exhibition of Angola Veterans Museum in Moscow. Next to "Liberdade" Vadim Sagachko, Andrei Tokarev, Sergei Kolomnin. April 15, 2018. Photo: S. Balakleyev

★224

NO CORAÇÃO DO POVO ANGOLANO

★226

★225. Members of the delegation of Union of Angola Veterans Nikolai Rybchuk (centre) and Andrei Tokarev, Ph.D. (History) among foreign participants of the 2nd International Colloquium on MPLA History held in Luanda on December 4–6, 2019. On the placard there is an inscription in Portuguese: "In the Heart of Angolan People" and the symbol of MPLA movement. December 6, 2019. Luanda. Photo: N. Rybchuk

★226. Members of the Union's delegation: Vice-Governor of the Tula Region Yuri Andrianov (left) and Vice-President of the Union of Angola Veterans Sergei Kolomnin with the Commander-in-Chief of Angola's Air Force Gen Francisco Afonso "Hanga" at the Luanda aifield before flying to Menongue in order to install a monument to fallen Soviet pilots in Angola. September 23, 2015. Photo: A. Stvolin

★227. Head of the Union's Naval Division Marine Col Sergei Remizov (left) talks to the guests of the photo exhibition "Angola. An important milestone". November 2015. Photo centre of the Union of Journalists on Gogolevsky Boulevard. Photo: S. Balakleyev

★227

★228

★228. The Union's photo exhibition "Angola.
An important milestone" in November 2015
was frequently attended by Angolan students
of Russian higher military schools.
Photo: A. Kalmykov

★229. Angola's veterans of the 369th Military
Transport Aviation Regiment of the USSR
Air Force were invited by the unit's command
to the ceremonial commemoration event
at the monument to "Aviators: Defenders
and Liberators of the Crimea"[52] in Dzhankoy.
The event marked the first anniversary
of deploying the recreated helicopter regiment
of the Russian Air Force on the Dzhankoy
airbase. July 24, 2016. Photo: N. Shurygin

★230. Veterans of the 369th Military Transport Aviation
Regiment of the USSR Air Force and relatives
of the fallen lay floral tributes to monument
to the pilots of An-12 plane, side number 11747,
shot down on November 25, 1985 in Angola.
November 25, 2010. Dzhankoy.
Photo: N. Shurygin

★229

★232

★**231.** On June 20, 2011 the Union of Angola Veterans organized a meeting of relatives of Soviet fighters-internationalists killed in the line of duty in Angola and Mozambique with Igor Sechin, Russia's Vice-Premier, and State Duma Member Vladimir Gruzdev (sitting to the right in the middle of the table). At the meeting forms and schedules of helping the families of the fallen were agreed. State Duma, Moscow. Photo: Union of Angola Veterans archive

★**232.** Angola veteran, Hero of Russia, Merited Test Pilot of the Russian Federation Ruben Esayan who was crew commander of the Yak-40 plane of Angola's Minister of Defense Pedro. M. T. "Pedale" in 1981–1984 talks to Sergei Kolomnin after receiving the badge of the Union of Angola Veterans. November 6, 2015. Photo: S. Balakleyev

★233

★234

★235

★236

★237

★233. Aleksei Pobortsev talks with the Angolan witness of the crash of An-12, side number 11747, in Angola. September 25, 2015, near Menongue. Photo: A. Stvolin

★234. Vadim Sagachko and Viktor Shalnev conduct a tour of the photo exhibition "Angola. An important milestone" for Angolan students of Russian military schools. November 2015, Moscow. Photo: A. Kalmykov

★235. Sergei Bogdanov who was one of the first to be decorated with the medal "For Internationalist Assistance to Angola" speaks about his trip to Angola. November 16, 2011. Photo: A. Kalmykov

★236. Opening of the Union's photo exhibition *We Could Not Have Been There* From left to right: Viacheslav Tetyokin, Member of the State Duma, Ambassador Extraordinary and Plenipotentiary Aleksandr Dzasokhov, Pyotr Suslov, veteran of Cascade and Vympel KGB groups. Moscow. June 4, 2009. Photo: S. Balakleyev

★237. Nikolai Shurygin, head of the Dzhankoy Union office (centre) holds a presentation of the first edition of the book *We Carried Out Our Duty. Angola: 1975–1992* at the local municipal library. 2016. Photo: N. Shurygin

★238

★239

★240

★238. A number of presentations of printed publications and films about Angola by Aleksei Pobortsev were held in Dzhankoy (Crimea) under the title "Years Spent in Angola". 2016. Photo: N. Shurygin (sitting, second left)

★239. The son of Col Nikolai Kurushkin, chief of the group of Soviet military specialists at SWAPO in Angola, Aleksandr Kurushkin (currently representative of the RF Chamber of Commerce and Industry in Namibia), at the Memorial Independence Museum in Windhoek near the stand with the photo of his father on which he is shown together with Peter Nanyemba, the legendary PLAN commander. 2019. Photo: S. Scripnik

★240. Vadim Sagachko presents the medal "For Internationalist Assistance to Angola" to the veteran of Angola, Warrant Officer (Ret.) V. Saliyev. 2014. Photo: A. Kalmykov

★241. Vadim Sagachko with heads of the Union offices in the Crimea and Sevastopol Aleksandr Bobovsky (centre) and in Novosibirsk Region Sergei Likhosherstov (right).

★242

★243

★242. Vadim Sagachko welcomes Admiral Julio Silva,
Military Attaché of Angola's Embassy in Moscow
who came to congratulate Russian veterans
of Angola on the 15th anniversary of the Union's
creation. November 16, 2019. Moscow.
Photo: S. Balakleyev

★243. The gala concert on the occasion
of the 15th anniversary of the foundation
of Union of Angola Veterans featured
both professional actors and Angola veterans
who sang their own songs. The photo shows
Aleksandr Grigorovich singing "Angolan Waltz".
November 16, 2019. Photo: S. Balakleyev

★244. After the ceremonial color guard presentation
sounds the Union of Angola Veterans' anthem.
November 16, 2019. Concert-hall of the
"Borodino-Hall" Hotel, celebration
of the 15th anniversary of the Union of Angola
Veterans. Moscow. Photo: S. Balakleyev

СОЮЗ В

★**245.** During the celebration of the 15th anniversary of the Union of Angola Veterans the most active veterans from the Union's regional offices were awarded the medal "For Assistance to Union of Angola Veterans". November 16, 2019. Concert-hall of the "Borodino-Hall" Hotel, Moscow. Photo: S. Balakleyev

★**246.** Sergei Timokhin, head of the fraternal organization – The Union of Syria Veterans (right) handed over a congratulatory address on the occasion of the 15th anniversary of the Union of Angola Veterans to Vadim Sagachko. November 16, 2019. Photo: S. Balakleyev

★**247.** Angolan and Cuban students of Moscow's higher schools congratulated the veterans at the gala concert on the occasion of 15 years since the foundation of the Union. November 16, 2019. Photo: S. Balakleyev

★246

★247

ПОМНИМ О ПРОШЛОМ,
ЖИВЁМ НАСТОЯЩИМ,
С УВЕРЕННОСТЬЮ
СМОТРИМ В БУДУЩЕЕ!

★249

★**248.** Joaquim Augusto de Lemos, Angola's Ambassador Extraordinary and Plenipotentiary in Russia who came to congratulate Russian veterans of Angola on the 15th anniversary of the Union together with the guests and organizers of the festive event on November 16, 2019. Concert hall of the "Borodino-Hall" Hotel, Moscow. Photo: S. Balakleyev

★**249.** Commemorative picture

★**250.** Luanda at night

144

Reference

1   **"To Defenders of Cuito Cuanavale"– a memorial exhibition complex** built in the 2000ies in the Angolan village of Cuito Cuanavale to commemorate the well-known Battle for Cuito Cuanavale 1987–1988 which stopped the advance of South African apartheid regime troops into the heart of Angola. The victory of Angolan-Cuban troops in the battle played a decisive role in liberating all territories occupied by South Africa and granting independence to Namibia.

2   **UNITA – National Union for the Total Independence of Angola** – a nationalist movement of Angola based on tribal principles, in 1975–2002 fought against MPLA and FAPLA, was strongly supported by the USA and some Western countries. In 2002 after the death of its intractable leader J. Savimbi, UNITA signed a ceasefire agreement with the government of Angola and became a legal political opposition party. UNITA has its faction in the country's parliament.

3   **FAPLA – National Front for the Liberation of Angola** (Forças Armadas Populares de Libertacão de Angola), the armed wing of MPLA, the army founded on August 1, 1974 on the basis of MPLA guerrilla detachments. On October 9, 1991 as a result of the reorganization and partial merger with UNITA armed forces were transformed into depoliticized armed forces of Angola. (FAA, Forças Armadas Angolanas).
MPLA – Popular Movement for the Liberation of Angola. Was later transformed into **the Labor Party**, Angola's political party, conducted national-liberation war against Portuguese colonizers. Its leadership was most consistent in the liberation of the country from colonial dependency through armed struggle, proclamation of national independence, building up a just society, free from racial discrimination and social exploitation in a united, independent country. It was guided by Marxist values and relied on the assistance of socialist countries and progressive representatives of liberated third world countries. On behalf of the Angolan people the MPLA proclaimed the country's independence on November 11, 1975 and since then has been the ruling party.

4   **Chief Military Adviser** – position created by the USSR Ministry of Defense in foreign countries which received comprehensive military aid from the Soviet Union. At the same time this person was chief of the group of Soviet military specialists in the country. In Angola these positions were occupied at different times by: Maj Gen I. F. Ponomarenko (1976–1977); Lt Gen V. V. Shakhnovich (1977–1980); Lt Gen G. S. Petrovsky (1980–1982); Col Gen K. Ya. Kurochkin (1982–1985); Lt Gen Kuzmenko (1985–1987); Lt Gen P. I. Gusev(1987–1990); Maj Gen S. A. Surodeyev (from April to November 1990); Lt Gen V. N. Belyaev (acting chief military adviser from November 1990 to February 1991). From 1991 the position of chief military adviser in Angola was called "Chief Military Consultant of Angola's Ministry of Defense". In 1991–1993 it was held by Lt Gen V. M. Lebedev.

5   **BDK** (Russian abbreviation) – Large Landing Ship.

6   **SWAPO – South West Africa People's Organization**, a military and political movement struggling for the liberation of Namibia. By agreement with the government of independent Angola in 1977–1990 its military bases and training centers were stationed in its territory. Since 1991 has been in power in independent Namibia.

7   **Up to the end of the 1980ies in Angola** the air wing of the Chief military adviser included about 12 turboprop An-12 planes which later were replaced with turbojet Il-76 military cargo planes. With Aeroflot identification marks on board they transported cargo and personnel in the interests of Soviet military specialists, FAPLA and Cuban troops. The first An-12 planes of the air wing started their operations in Angola from 1976 and by the end of the 80ies about twenty military and transport planes manned by Soviet crews works in the country.

8   **BPK** (Russian abbreviation) – Large ASW Ship.

9   **The USSR Navy 30th Operations Brigade** – a task force of the Soviet Navy set up in the 70–80ies from the group of surface ships, submarines and auxiliary vessels of the Northern, Baltic and Black Sea fleets operating in the Atlantic. The main bases were Conakri (Guinea Republic) and Luanda, the port of the capital of Angola. The brigade's operating support in Luanda was rendered by a specially created 877th Naval Facility with units on Angolan Naval and Air Force bases. Every year the Naval Facility in Luanda served up to 20 visiting surface and fleet-support ships, about two or three submarines (including nuclear powered), received, served and let out up to 50 combat reconnaissance planes Tu-95RTs of marine aviation and An-12 and Il-76 tactical support planes. The Headquarters of the 30th Brigade as well as those of the 5th Operations Squadron were based in the Mediterranean on the ships which were under the command of the 30th Brigade for the period of operational service. The 30th Brigade was under the direct command of the USSR Navy General Staff.

10 **SVS** (Russian abbreviation) – Soviet military specialists, **SVSiS** (Russian abbreviation) – Soviet military specialists and advisers. Abbreviations used by the 10th Chief Directorate of the USSR General Staff in relation to Soviet military specialists stationed abroad to work in the armies of developing countries.

11 **Long-range marine reconnaissance plane Tu-95RTs** was at the time one of the main aircraft for detecting submarines and US aircraft carriers in the world ocean. On the Atlantic theatre these tasks were the responsibility of the personnel of the 392th Separate Long-Range Reconnaissance Aviation Regiment whose crews in the 70–80ies made regular reconnaissance flights on Tu-95RTs using airfields of Havana, Conakri and Luanda for stopovers.

12 **"Sovispan" – a joint Soviet-Spanish trade and procurement company** with the headquarters on the Canary Islands (Las-Palmas). It supplied the Soviet military advisers abroad and crews of Soviet combat and auxiliary vessels with food and consumer goods.

13 **Joáo Lourenço, future President of Angola** (elected in 2017), studied in Moscow at the Lenin Military Political Academy from 1978 to 1982, defended a dissertation in history. As of January 1, 1995 military higher schools of the USSR and Russia trained 6 985 qualified Angolan servicemen: among them 3 258 men for the army, for anti-aircraft personnel – 1 084, for the air force – 1 310 specialists, for the navy 591, and 104 logisticians and 638 specialists in other fields.

14 **On August 27, 1981** during yet another invasion of South African troops into the southern districts of Angola (Operation "Protea") **Soviet warrant officer Nikolai Pestretsov** was taken prisoner by the soldiers of the "Buffalo" battalion spending one and a half years in captivity. Pestretsov had been sent to Angola as a specialist in motor vehicles at the 11th Angolan Infantry Brigade defending Onjiva (Ongiva). South African mechanized units surrounded Onjiva. As a result of the battle in August 1981 four Soviet citizens were killed by South Africans: adviser of the brigade's chief of artillery Lt Col Yevgeny Kireyev, his wife Lidia Kireyeva, adviser of the brigade's political officer Lt Col Josif Vazhnik and N. Pestretsov's wife Galina Pestretsova. Pestretsov was freed only in November 1982 with two other Soviet citizens captured by the UNITA – Kamil Mollayev and Ivan Thernetsky as a result of an exchange for the South Africans captured in Angola.

15 **PLAN** – armed forces (army) set up by SWAPO with the help of Soviet military advisers and specialists. In Angola three PLAN brigades were organized, trained and armed with Soviet weapons. They later formed a nucleus for creating armed forces of independent Namibia. In the 70–80ies PLAN units fought on the territory of South West Africa (Namibia) against South African occupational forces and also took part in FAPLA combat operations against the UNITA armed opposition inside Angola.

16 After **K. Kurochkin had completed his mission to Angola as the Chief Military Advisor** he continued to supervise Angolan affairs in the USSR Ministry of Defense visiting Angola several times as head of working

groups of the General Staff in order to render assistance to the Angolan side. In 1987 when the situation in Angola deteriorated the Cuban leader F. Castro invited K. Kurochkin to Havana to discuss the coordination of Cuban and Soviet sides in the battle of Cuito Cuanavale in Angola.

17 **Cuban pilots** Lt Col Manuel Rojas Garcia and Capt Ramon Quesada Aguilara who flew MIG-21UM training plane were shot down on October 28, 1987 by the UNITA surface-to-air missile. They were captured by the UNITA militants who subsequently used them for propaganda purposes. The pilots were released as a result of peaceful negotiations in August 24, 1988. Manuel Rojas Garcia later wrote a book about these events – *UNITA Prisoners in the End of the Earth* which was published both in Spanish and Portuguese.

18 **In the early hours of June 6, 1986 in the port of Namibe combat South African swimmers** mined and exploded Soviet dry cargo ships *Kapitan Chirkov* (16 000 tonnage) and *Kapitan Vislobokov* (12 000 tonnage) which had delivered about 20,000 tons of weapons and ammunition for the Angolan army, SWAPO guerrillas and ANC, as well as the Cuban ship (6 000 tonnage) *Habana* with the cargo of food and ammunition. Soviet vessels managed to retain buoyancy, but on their underbodies activated mines were found. A group of combat swimmers of the Black Sea Navy Underwater Sabotage Group under Yuri Plyachenko, Capt 2nd rank, was brought to Namibe by a charter plane. Together with a group of frogmen of the ASW ship *Stroinyi* under the command of Sen Lt Maksim Ivanov they managed to remove the undetonated mines from the boards of Soviet ships and thus save them. As a result of that operation three officers from the Plyachenko group were awarded the Order of Red Star, the rest were decorated with the medals "For Distinguished Military Service". Maksim Ivanov who spent the total of 24 hours under water was too decorated with the Order of Red Star.

19 **In August 1981** as a result of armed invasion of the South African troops into the southern districts of Angola were occupied the towns of Onjiva (Ongiva) , Xangongo and Cahama. During this period South Africans killed four Soviet citizens and captured one.

20 **On November 25, 1985 Soviet military transport plane An-12**, side number 11747, from the 369th Military Transport Regiment of the USSR Air Force (permanent base Dzhankoy) flying under the "Aeroflot" flag was shot down in Angola in the area of Menongue. The missile was launched by the task force RECCES of South African special forces. Eight members of the crew were killed: Commander Capt Sergei Lukyanov, Sen Lt Viktor Osadchuk, Lt Vitaly Pshenyuk, warrant officer Sergei Grishenkov, Warrant Officer Vladimir Shibanov and translator, student of the Military Institute of Foreign Languages of the Ministry of Defense Sergei Sholmov. Among those killed on board there were four Soviet military advisers: Col Yevgeny Kandidatov, Lt Cols Alexander Martynov, Mikhail Zhernosek and Anatoly Perevertov as well as eight Angolan officers.

21 **Chief Political Directorate of the Soviet Army and Navy**.

22 **FAPA** – Força Aêria Popular de Angola (Portuguese), the Angolan Air Force.

23 **DAA** – Defesa Anti-Aêria (Portuguese), the Angolan Air Defense Forces.

24 **MLRS** – multiple launch rocket system.

25 **Four MLRS BM-21 "Grad"** which played a decisive role in the MPLA's victory at the Battle of Quifangondo were brought from the USSR to the Congolese port Pointe Noire on military transport planes An-22 ("Antey") of the 12th Mginsk Military Transport Division. The flight and landing at Pointe Noire took place in extremely hard meteorological conditions, with limited airborne weight (short unpaved airstrip). Later on November 7, 1975 the systems were transported to Luanda from Pointe Noire and in the early hours of November 10 secretly delivered to Quifangondo.

26 **FNLA – the National Liberation Front of Angola**, Angolan nationalist movement. Its predecessor – the Union of Peoples of Northern Angola (UPNA) was founded by the representatives of protestant nobility of Bacongo, an African tribe (living by the way on the territory of modern Angola) as an ethnic, separatist organization whose primary goal was to unite the Angolan Bacongo around the idea of the recreation of "a great state of Congo". It took an active part in the war for independence and civil war in Angola. In the 70–80ies it fought against the MPLA and FAPLA, from 1992 – the right political party. Traditionally supported by the Bacongo nationality and occupied conservative tribal positions.

27 **The lost crew and the helicopter belonged to** the Myachkovo Joint Squadron of the Moscow Civil Aviation Administration of the USSR, which worked in Angola under a contract with the Ministry of Geodesy and Cartography of Angola, performing topographic surveys. Four crew members, two members of the topographic party and the son of the party chief were killed in the crash. The lengthy search for the site of the crash failed to bring any results. For a long time the people on board were considered missing. It was only in January 1989 when the wreckage of the helicopter was discovered in a difficult-to-reach area 140 km north of Luanda. In May 1989, the remains of the killed Soviet citizens were transported to Moscow. The examination of the damage to the helicopter showed that it had been shot down from the ground by small arms. (Source: Order No. 200 of November 30, 1989 of the USSR Ministry of Civil Aviation).

28 **In the 70–80ies over 20 warships were delivered from the USSR to Angola** in order to set up national naval forces, among them: six 205ER missile boats, four 206 torpedo boats, three 771 medium landing ships, a 1400ME "Griff" border patrol boat, three 368P patrol boats, two 1398B "Aist" boats, as well as two 1258B minesweepers.

29 **Peter Nanyemba (1935–1983)** – Commander of the People's Liberation Army of Namibia (PLAN) during the war of independence – earlier had been known as a successful diplomat representing SWAPO in Botswana

and Tanzania. In 1970 he was elected SWAPO's Secretary for Defence. In 1983 he died in a car accident in Angola. The SWAPO Field Hospital near the Angolan city of Lubango was named after him – the Peter Nanyemba Military Hospital. National Hero of Namibia.

30 **Operation "Carlota"** – transfer of Cuban troops to Angola to rebuff the external aggression and help the Angolan MPLA movement. Conducted in 1975–1976 at the request of MPLA leadership, it was retaliation by the MPLA and Cuba for the open military intervention of South Africa and Zaire in Angola. The transfer of troops and equipment from Cuba was carried out by Cuban transport vessels Vietnam Heroico, *El Corals Islands* and *La Plata*, Cuban Civil Aviation Bristol-Britannia planes as well as Soviet civilian ships and Il-62 aircraft.

31 **The Battle of Quifangondo (23.10–10.11, 1975)** – the major battle of the war for Angola's independence in which the MPLA armed detachments and Cuban internationalists defeated the troops of the FNLA and Zaire advancing on Luanda. The defeat of the armed opposition and foreign interventionists near Quifangondo helped the MPLA to retain control over Luanda and on the night of November 11, 1975, it proclaimed the independence of Angola. The battle got its name from the place of hostilities – the Quifangondo settlement and area (another spelling is Kifangondo) a few kilometers north of Luanda near the Bengo River.

32 **In November 2007**, on the initiative of Vyacheslav Petrovich Kozlov, head of the Kolomna office of the Union of Angola Veterans, member of the Board of the Kolomna branch of the Moscow regional organization "The Moscow Region Invalids", veteran of the Afghanistan and Angola wars, a Grove of Memory as a symbol of friendship between the soldiers of Russia and Angola was planted near Kolomna, at the confluence of the Repinka River with the Kolomenka River. The first two pines were planted by Angola veterans V. P. Kozlov, V. A. Patrin., V. A. Bersenev and the commander of the artillery of the Angolan Armed Forces, graduate of the RF General Staff Academy Lt Gen Antonio José de Sousa Queiroz, who came

to visit them with his family. In 2018, a memorial stone with the inscription "Grove in Memory of Those Killed in Local Conflicts" was solemnly installed in the grove with the participation of local authorities. Memorial events and reunions of veterans are regularly held in the grove, floral tributes and wreaths are laid on the stone on holidays and memorable days.

33 **Military Training and Research Center of the Air Force** "Air Force Academy named after Professor N. Ye. Zhukovsky and Yu. A. Gagarin".

34 Joáo E. dos Santos "Liberdade" was appointed Minister of Defense and Veterans Affairs of Angola by **Decree No. 26/20 of March 26, 2020 of the President of the Republic of Angola**.

35 **General Simão Carlitos Wala** is a legendary figure in the modern history of Angola. He is known both in Angola and Russia as well as throughout the world as commander of the Angolan Armed Forces (FAA) operation codenamed "Kissonde" ("Ant"). In February 2002 this operation led to the elimination of General Jonas Malheiro Savimbi, the implacable leader of the armed Angolan opposition and head of UNITA and FALA (UNITA Armed Forces). During the FAA operation starting in 1999 and lasting for three years (codename "Restauração" ("Restoration"), Savimbi's troops were ousted from the provinces of Lunda-Norte and Lunda-Sul, Huambo, Bié, Malange and most of Mexico. The former main base and the UNITA "capital", Jamba, were also taken over. But the decisive blow to Savimbi was dealt by the 20th Brigade of the Angolan army under the command of General Wala. On February 22, 2002, the implacable leader of UNITA was overtaken, surrounded and killed in the province of Mexico near the Lungué Bungo (Lungwebungu) River by the brigade's special forces unit. After his death, the military organization UNITA began to fall apart like a "house of cards" and the war was practically over.

36 **Military Academy of the RF Armed Forces General Staff**.

37 **The 392nd Separate Long-Range Reconnaissance Aviation Regiment of the Air Force of the Northern Fleet** was based at the Kipelovo airfield (now Fedotovo, Vologda Region). It was from there that in the 70–80ies Tu-95RTs reconnaissance aircraft flew combat missions to Cuba and Angola.

38 During his visit to Cuba in February 2013 **the Russian Prime Minister Dmitry Medvedev** at the request of the Council of the Union presented Fidel Castro Ruz with the badge of the honorary member of the Union of Angola Veterans and the medal "For Internationalist Assistance to Angola".

39 **Military transport aviation regiment**.

40 **In June 2016, during the visit by a group of Angola veterans to the Valaam Monastery's Temple of Military Memory**, thanks to the efforts of Svetlana Polyakova, Union's coordinator of the project "Chronicle of Activities of Civilian Specialists-Internationalists in Angola", it was agreed that the monks would accept for "the eternal prayer" all those Soviet and Russian specialists and their spouses who were killed or died while performing their official and internationalist duty in Angola.

41 **Higher military aviation school for pilots**.

42 **Barry Fowler, former captain of the South African Defence Force Medical Service**, donated his military uniform in which he served in the South African units on the border of Namibia and Angola in the mid-80ies to the Museum of the Union of Angola Veterans.

43 **Former commander of the 4th reconnaissance and sabotage detachment of the South African Defence Force (4 Recce) Douw Steyn** visited Moscow in July 2016 on the occasion of the release of the documentary film *Confessions of a Russian sailor. They wanted to blow me up*. The film tells the story of Maksim Ivanov,

Russian naval mariner and Angola veteran, who in 1986 took part in the removal of mines from Soviet civilian ships *Kapitan Chirkov* and *Kapitan Vislobokov*. Douw Steyn who then fought on the South African side participated in this sabotage mining operation code-named "Drozdi." During the meeting in the Union of Angola Veterans, in addition to the magazines, Douw Steyn received a gift – the book by S. Kolomnin *We Have Carried Out Our Duty. Angola: 1975–1992*, some other publications of the Union and several unique photos from the Union's archives taken by Soviet military advisers depicting appalling results of the activities of South African Recces in Angola. The meeting turned out to be extremely productive as it helped clarify details of many acts of sabotage committed by South Africa in the territory of Angola in the 70ies and 80ies and countermeasures by FAPLA and the staff of Soviet military advisers in Angola.

44 **ANC – African National Congress of South Africa** – the oldest political organization of South African people (founded in 1912), acted in alliance with the Congress of South African Trade Unions (COSATU) and the South African Communist Party. At the end of the 20th century struggled for the elimination of the disgraceful system of apartheid, including by military force. The ANC operations on the territory of the country were illegal, with its training bases located abroad, in Angola among others. The ANC personnel and its military wing "Umkhontowesizwe" ("uMkontove Sizve", "The Spear of the Nation") in Angola were trained exclusively by Soviet military specialists.

45 **More about V. Shiryaev's activities in Angola** to be found in the book by S. Kolomnin *We Have Carried Out Our Duty. Angola 1975–1992*, M .: Studio 'Ethnica' publishing house (IP Troshkov A. V.), 2018.– p.: 296 ISBN 978-5-9907693-9-7, pp.1 72–175.

46 **A. Tokarev, Ph.D (History) made a report** on the assistance of the USSR and Russia to the Angolan people in the struggle for freedom, independence and territorial integrity of the country at the 2nd International Colloquium on the History of the MPLA held in Luanda on December 4–6, 2019.

47 **Sergei Grigoriyev has been decorated with the badge "For Assistance to the Union of Angola Veterans".** This badge is awarded for important personal contribution to the solution of tasks facing the organization.

48 **The capture of Kamil Mollaev** and his release is described in the book by Sergei Kolomnin *We Have Carried Out Our Duty. Angola: 1975–1992*, M .: Studio 'Ethnica' publishing house (IP Troshkov A. V.), 2018.– p.: 296 ISBN 978-5-9907693-9-7, pp. 218–231, as well as on the Union website *http: // www. veteranangola. ru/main/history/pailot_history*

49 **Yevgeny Kalinin. Separate long-range reconnaissance.** From the history of the 392nd ODRAP of the Northern Fleet. Cherepovets. 2013. ISBN 978-5-9904634-1-7.

50 **Military personnel of the South African ANC** and its military wing "Umkhonto we Sizwe" ("The Spear of the nation") in the 70-80ies were trained in Angola by Soviet military specialists.

51 **Memoirs of Tatiana Ivanovna Khudoyerko** "He Who Says that the War is Not Scary Has Not Seen the War" published in the book by S. Kolomnin *We Have Carried Out Our Duty. Angola: 1975–1992*, M.: Studio 'Ethnica' publishing house (IP Troshkov A. V.), 2018.– p.: 296 ISBN 978-5-9907693-9-7, pp.152–163.

52 **The monument "To Aviators: Defenders and Liberators of the Crimea"** was erected to mark the 20th Anniversary of the Victory of the Soviet people in the Great Patriotic War of 1941–1945. Unveiled May 9, 1965.

**СОЮЗ
ВЕТЕРАНОВ
АНГОЛЫ**

Russian Veterans of Angola:
from the Past to Nowadays

PHOTO ALBUM

Compiled by: Sergey Kolomnin, Sergey Balakleyev.
Photos from the Archives of the Union of Angola Veterans,
collection of reports by Vladislav Dmitriyenko
Angola: the Road of Struggle and Labor.

Translated by Igor Kalyonov

M.: Studio 'Ethnica' publishing house (IP Troshkov A.V.).

14+

Signed to print 20.09.2020. Format 290x220.
Coated paper. Offset printing. Font «Helvetica».
Cond. sheets19,0. Circulation: 1000 copies.

Printed in accordance with the materials provided

ISBN 978-5-6045476-1-8

© Kolomnin Sergei Anatolyevich, 2020 © Balakleyev Sergei Aleksandrovich, 2020 © Design: Ethnica studio, 2020